SELECTED POEMS

To Janet,

BERNARD O'DONOGHUE

Selected Poems

with all good wishes

and thanks,

Bernard O' Donoghue

Clairmont, 3/11/2011

ff

faber and faber

First published in 2008
by Faber and Faber Limited
3 Queen Square London WC1N 3AU

Typeset by Faber and Faber Limited
Printed in England by T. J. International Ltd, Padstow, Cornwall
Printed on FSC accredited material

The author wishes to thank Chatto & Windus and The Gallery Press
for the original publication of these poems

The right of Bernard O'Donoghue to be identified as author
of this work has been asserted in accordance with Section 77
of the Copyright, Designs and Patents Act 1988

Reproduced by kind permission of Chatto & Windus,
Random House, 20 Vauxhall Bridge Road,
London SW1V 2SA

A CIP record for this book
is available from the British Library

ISBN 978-0-571-23638-1

2 4 6 8 10 9 7 5 3 1

Contents

from OUTLIVING (2003)

from
THE WEAKNESS

A Nun Takes the Veil

That morning early I ran through briars
To catch the calves that were bound for market.
I stopped the once, to watch the sun
Rising over Doolin across the water.

The calves were tethered outside the house
While I had my breakfast: the last one at home
For forty years. I had what I wanted (they said
I could), so we'd loaf bread and Marie biscuits.

We strung the calves behind the boat,
Me keeping clear to protect my style:
Confirmation suit and my patent sandals.
But I trailed my fingers in the cool green water,

Watching the puffins driving homeward
To their nests on Aran. On the Galway mainland
I tiptoed clear of the cow-dunged slipway
And watched my brothers heaving the calves

As they lost their footing. We went in a trap,
Myself and my mother, and I said goodbye
To my father then. The last I saw of him
Was a hat and jacket and a salley stick,

Driving cattle to Ballyvaughan.
He died (they told me) in the county home,
Asking to see me. But that was later:
As we trotted on through the morning mist,

I saw a car for the first time ever,
Hardly seeing it before it vanished.
I couldn't believe it, and I stood up looking
To where I could hear its noise departing

But it was only a glimpse. That night in the convent
The sisters spoilt me, but I couldn't forget
The morning's vision, and I fell asleep
With the engine humming through the open window.

O'Regan the Amateur Anatomist

The gander clapped out its flat despair
While O'Regan sawed at its legs with his penknife.
He looked at me with a friendly smile as blood
Dripped in huge, dark drips. I didn't protest
Or flail out at him, but smiled in return,
Knowing what grown-ups do, whatever breeds
About their hearts, is always for the best.
Worms are cold-blooded; babies learn in the night
By being left to cry. Another time (a man
So generous, they said, he'd give you the sweet
From his mouth) he halved a robin with that knife.
Finally, racing his brother back from a funeral
Down a darkening road he drove his car
Under a lightless lorry, cutting his head off.
I wonder what he thought he was up to then?

Finn the Bonesetter

Proverbial wisdom kept us off the streets
And that's a fact. The art of talk is dead.
When we had shaken all our heads enough
At people's knowing in the days of old
(When a cow died they thanked Almighty God
It wasn't one of them), we'd contemplate
Our local marvel-workers. On the flat
Of his back for three years and more, surgeons
Could do nothing: Finn had him walking
The four miles to Mass inside an hour.

Incurably rheumatical myself,
I made him out at home above Rockchapel
Where the swallows purred approving in the eaves.
Bent at a crystal mirror, he was bathing
A red eye. 'I'm praying I won't go blind
From it. Do you know anything about eyes?'
Beyond having heard it said that his descried
The future, I didn't. He rolled his sleeves
Back to his shoulder like an accredited
Inseminator and got down to it.
I'm much relieved and think there's something in it.

Pisheogue Master

Tonight by the hearth the wind gave up the ghost,
Letting the ash drift and signalling
Unventilated blight-mist in the morning,

Good for my purpose. So I'll take the eggs,
Abandoned by the hen who was laying out
Under the blackthorn. There they sat for months,

Snuffed nightly by the hungry fox and left,
Thirteen cold *gliogars* with the reassuring scent
Of H_2S. I must not see myself

As I fold the rancid butter in my coat
And slide from its sock the orange-bottle, full
Of slime-twining water from the sick calf's bed.

Everything must be said and nothing seen.
Sprinkle the water on the boundary fence;
Smear the butter on the pumptree. Listen (shush!)

To their child wheezing as her chest constricts:
My ill-luck, maybe, already on the wing.
Tuck up the loveless eggs in my rotting hay

To make a swaddling-bundle with soft words
And bear it past the hedges to bequeath
Its damp heat deep in the neighbouring barns.

Then tomorrow I'll look all men in the eye,
Despising their priestly superstitions and
Their cowering aspersions on my faith.

The air begins to brighten. In the tree
The thrush is wakened up by his own singing.
Stealing home unmissed, I notice the stone

Supporting my slumped gate has rolled away.
I see these things as omens and take hope;
If my sick wife should die, I'd die of grief.

Immaturities

My Manchester mother was a City fan,
So I'm one too. Once, as Wembley sang
'Abide With Me' (only, my father said,
Upsetting people), she shockingly
Ran crying from our Irish kitchen.

But when, that February, ice on the wing
Caused the United plane to crash,
Club differences were dropped. Cuttings came
From the *Evening News* about the Sheffield match,
Reporting 'a ghost in every red shirt'.

The milk-windows of ice cracked beneath
Our heels as we, local celebrities,
Walked to the shop. – Was our mother upset? –
Not really. (You couldn't admit as much.)
There was another, similar vapouring

When Regan set the black dog swinging
From the friesian's tail. Her hind legs splayed
In the dust, making her ample milk-bag
Look ridiculous. My mother clutched her ears
And stamped and screamed. Such a display in public!

And then, when my father died, we wondered
Driving home if those half-hushed night arguments
Meant she'd take it with indifference.
But when we opened the door, we thought the noise
That greeted us was a mad cow roaring.

Made in England

The pulper still outside the window
Blocking the light, twenty years since
Its handle turned and the last droppings
Fell from it. 'English stuff costs more' –
Tracing the cast-iron, proud legend
Bamford – 'but it lasts the longest.
Like the BSA frame, guaranteed
For ever.' But few in this inch
Of Atlantean West Cork
Could stay the pace with it.

Tom's Soldiers

A humming Gulliver, spreadeagled in
The carpet's geometry, surrounded
By plastic personnel with arms levelled:
Two hundred plus, ten per 90p platoon,
And reinforced weekly. His thoughtful heels
Kick out a strategy, accompanied
By quiet, palatal-fricative explosions.

But where will it end? The obsessional,
If I remember rightly, continues
With football; stamp-collecting; God; the dog;
Music; sex; and our present crotchety,
Opinionated lives. Farther than that
I can't predict for him, still waiting myself
For reason's horses to declare the outcome.

The Apparition

More surprising than a moving statue
Of the Blessed Virgin, that yellow plane
Stationary in an Irish farmer's field
In the Fifties: a four-day shrine until
Its tilted take-off, a wing-heavy heron.

That wasn't the end of it: disputation
Ran for months about its origins: what age
It came from, or what place; in what hangar
It wintered, north or south; whether our climate
Was too hot or cold for it: too dry or wet.

Last night I dreamt I saw it once again,
Thirty years later, on an empty patch
Beside the jumbo runway at Heathrow
From the window of a transatlantic jet
Through the pre-departure gauze of heat.

I tried to call 'what message have you brought
From Bill Casey's field?' But the Boeing's whine
Defeated me as it carefully conducted
Its slow, elephantine pirouette.
Accepting that I'd never hear the truth,

I settled back to study our flight-path;
But as we drifted past it, gathering speed,
I saw clearly the notice I'd forgotten
Chalked on cardboard in the pilot's seat:
'Out of fuel. Back when we've got some more'.

The State of the Nation

*The condition upon which God hath given
liberty to man is eternal vigilance.*
JOHN PHILPOT CURRAN, 1790

Before I fell asleep, I had been reading
How in the Concentration Camps, alongside
The Jewish personal effects, were stored
For future reference gipsies' earrings,
Scarves and the crystal globes in which they saw
The future; and how the Guardia Civil
Swept through Fuente Vaqueros, smashing guitars.

The book was open still when I woke up
At dawn and, not reassured by the May chorus
From the cypresses, ran to the encampment
At the crossroads where slow smoke curled by the sign
'Temporary Dwellings Prohibited'.
Still there; spread in dew along the hedges
Were gossamer and shawls and tea-towels.

A chained dog watched me peering under
The first canvas flap. Empty. The rest the same.
Not a soul in any tent. I straightened up
And listened through the sounds of morning
For voices raised in family rows, or their ponies
Tocking back from venial raids, bringing home
Hay, a clutch of eggs, unminded pullets.

The Usual Suspects

The patent stuff I spray on the flowers
Makes insects lose all reason. Instead
Of escaping, they leap at the nozzle
Till all their green cadavers lie soused
In their rosewood bedrooms. The roses
Are no better: they jag and tear at the hand
That risks the faecal dampness to pull out
The choking clover, bringing their roots air.

Last night's electric storm came just when their buds
Were opening and the peony's crimson egg
Was splitting to give birth. In the morning
The peony lies prone, the rosebuds shrivelled
And the dead greenfly are all washed away.
The clover prospers silently. It defeats
The roses to know who to blame, since
When you hear something, that's nothing.
When you hear nothing, that's the Indian.

The Saga of McGuinness's Dog

A man lived by the Araglen river
Called John Tim Jack. He kept the greyhounds for
The village doctor on his farm. The doctor,
As a man of substance, had a fridge before
The days of fridges, where he kept the dog-meat:
Bones, knuckles and unconvincing-looking
Daubs of red. John Tim's children tried to seize

The moment when the fridge light winked off.
The doctor, trundling in from his visits
To the pub, would list in the doorway, asking
'Are you sure the fridge light's out? Is the cow
Still in the grove?' Cows they knew well of old;
But the grove was attributed to drink
As they stole away and left him to reflect.

In February, when evenings first lengthened out,
School ended at two to let the scholars
Watch the coursing. John Tim brought the dogs,
Mad eyes and coats shining, lolling tongues
Looking too long to fit back in their heads.
They never won; but once his *Maggie's Fury*
Nearly made it. The children stood and cheered

Through the early rounds as hare after hare
Was ripped until the cold moon was noticed,
Rousing concern for dogs' legs in the frost.
Fury's opponent in the final had
A name (maybe false) no one had heard of,

Entered by a stranger calling himself
McGuinness, with coat collar turned up.

Another hare made in a doomed scuttle
For the grass curtain at the course's end.
Fury was off like lightning over the glint
Of frost-grass to take the first turn in style.
But *Tanyard Subject* came from nowhere, winning
The second. The hare was killed. *Fury* was kicked
Back in his trailer for the dark drive home.

The Nuthatch

I couldn't fathom why, one leafless
Cloudcast morning he appeared to me,
Taking time off from his rind-research
To spread his chestnut throat and sing
Outside my window. His woodwind
Stammering exalted every work-day
For weeks after. Only once more
I saw him, quite by chance, among
The crowding leaves. He didn't lift
His head as he pored over his wood-text.
Ashamed of the binocular intrusion,
Like breath on eggs or love pressed too far,
I'm trying to pretend I never saw him.

Bittern

Ultimately sex, no doubt: like a drunk's
Drooled elegy across the rounded lips
Of an empty bottle. Standing, kind of,
Chin in the air, thick head swaying in time
To the wind. Soliciting nobody
For nothing, a real non-combatant.
He's trying to pass like Syrinx for a reed,
A daft civilian in a daft disguise.
Out of touch with his leggy womenfolk,
Those symbols of longevity: the keen heron,
The stiletto-shod crane stilting archly
Round the puddles, the pink-gorged flamingo
Dropping off on one leg, bored with alluring.
He can't be serious! Does he really think
The fowler at the break of day
Will take him for a tender grass and go?

Morning in Beara

Towns, small islands, *domus* and *rus*
Is the rule in this last wedge of state
Sketched over by cartographers.
Angled houses through glassless frames
Overlook the sound where the gannet
Cuts out and falls. The curate
Developed a stammer; the economy
He founded foundered. His photos even
Were blurred, of this corner
Where no one comes on purpose.

Men came once, unwrapping bales
Of something on the beach. They glazed
The windows and repaired the thatch,
Starting a honey-farm in nine rows
Of cannabis. But the Council
Broke the windows, and in the rafters
Hung Vapona for the bees.

Back in the status quo, the old woman
Takes up her ageless beat again.
A mile or so out,
You can listen to the shingle's scramble
As the escaping pebbles lose their footing.

Souvenirs

'*Tá an lá go breá!*' 'You have the Irish well.
An bhfuil souvenirs uait? Here I have
Souvenirs my own hands made, from shells
Found westward on the Aran beaches,
Not on this island only, but as well
On Inishmean and Inishmore.'

He led me past his father who was sitting
In the sun, looking with the satisfaction
Of a tourist over the sea. Pieces
Of crooked copper wire (as it were Celtic
Torques, shrunken like toy dogs from the miracles
Displayed in the National Museum)

Were spread on his wiped kitchen oilcloth.
'Would souvenirs be pleasing to your wife
Or to your children? Children often like
Souvenirs.' All I had in my pocket
Smaller than fivers were three golden
English pounds, and I offered them.

'English money is all right too. We change
It for Irish in the Galway banks,
Or at the mobile bank that stops longside
The music pub in Doolin.' Now they're on a shelf
Here in my study, and all I can recall
Is wondering if his English came from Synge.

P.T.A.

'Parent Teacher Association'.
Ganging up on the innocent,
Sounds like to me. When Lear turns nasty –
'Take heed, sirrah! The whip!' –
I recognise the voice of those
Weird fathers who urged the teacher
'Give them the stick and plenty of it.'

Easy to talk, of course. Maybe
That was the best education
For their lives: suitcases
Upturned on customs desks;
Cross-examination by people,
Themselves fearful, who hate
Without understanding.

Holy Island

Bells ringing over the water
Make sweeter music and carry
More strongly to greater distance

At Mass time, when at home I'd escape
With rose clippings to the council dump,
I walked by the shore where turnstones
Rolled along the sand like a spilt rosary
And merry clouds of knot veered through the sea's
Splash of light, like guilt-arousing girls
On holiday with skirts tucked up,
Pushing, shrieking, linked at the elbow.

Across the shell-debris beach the island
Where the saint bestowed his soul.
Twice a day it edges towards the land
And backs away again, like a child learning fear,
Unsure of its welcome. Pilgrim cormorants,
Like stigmata-seekers, lift out their wings
Showing their blue-black, unsandalled feet.
No nightingale, no thrush in the blue evening
Will serenade this tattered cross
Tolling its barren silence over the sound.

The Potter's Field

With better luck he might have been a saint
Or, failing that, lived richly on the interest,
Since thirty silver pieces is a lot.
Yet he flung his fortune back on principle
And, weeping, ran away and hanged himself.
Hearing that tale the first time, any child
Might well, until instructed, cry at his fate.

So what made him the byword for a traitor,
Forever gnawed by thin-lipped Dante's Satan?
Observe the lettering above the gate:
'Iscariot's cemetery for foreign nationals'.
Bequests like his win no one love; their need's
Resented, like a prostitute's caress
Consigned by its beneficiary to Hell.

Somewhere near Rockall in the western ocean,
There is a crag that spits the Atlantic's spray
Back in its face. There, once a century,
Judas sits for the night, his lips refleshing
In the wind, craving the beads of water
He sees hang in every purple clapper
Down endless avenues of seaboard fuchsia.

My tears-of-god bloom as red here beside
The Queen Elizabeth and Iceberg roses
As on their native drywall back in Kerry.
The soil's hospitable; the air is delicate.
So I think that now I'm well enough heeled in
To rate a plot inside the graveyard wall,
Escaping Giudecca. Accursèd be his name!

The Weakness

It was the frosty early hours when finally
The cow's despairing groans rolled him from bed
And into his boots, hardly awake yet.
He called 'Dan! come on, Dan!
She's calving', and stumbled without his coat
Down the icy path to the haggard.

Castor and Pollux were fixed in line
Over his head but he didn't see them,
This night any more than another.
He crossed to the stall, past the corner
Of the fairy-fort he'd levelled last May.
But this that stopped him, like the mind's step

Backward: what was that, more insistent
Than the calf's birth-pangs? 'Hold on, Dan.
I think I'm having a weakness.
I never had a weakness, Dan, before.'
And down he slid, groping for the lapels
Of the shocked boy's twenty-year-old jacket.

Con Cornie

in memoriam

A farmer's fingers on a flageolet,
Bunched, too crowded, but weaving
A seamless tapestry of sound. A glide
Through a drift of touch, a slur conceded
By a wise, sideways moving of the head.

What complaint was stitched on to the air –
What child bereaved or wife sorrowing –
Was not his part now, intent on making
A fling of notes you could broadcast anywhere.

The Humours of Shrone

The peregrine's anxious *kai* hangs
In the air-bowl of the mountains
Over the limestone lake, water so black
That even in heatwave summer it dims
The sun. There, eighty years ago

On Christmas Eve our young neighbour pulled
His horse's jawing head
Into the blizzard for the eight miles
Of nodding, doddering at the reins
With his swirling load of quicklime.

The red candle in the window was burnt through,
Its warm hole in the frost veil closed
Before his sister heard in the haggard
The frenzied horse clashing his traces
Down the stone yard and the jagged

Shafts leaping behind, trying to keep up.
They found the boy next morning in our quarry
In the snow, with blind holes lime-burned in his face.
So the sister said: ninety, doting and inclined
To roam the quarry-field to search again.

Round the Campfire

The grassy bridge, cut off now
By the new road's sweep, is
My daughter's memorial:
The undergrowth still fused
To half-burnt tin and
Non-biodegradable plastic.

At Appleby she darted laughing
From the van, dodging hooves
Better than anyone. She sang
'Dingle Bay' all down the M1
On our way to run the gauntlet
Of the customs.

Why it was going to Puck Fair
She died, I couldn't say.
She knew the road well; she ran
No quicker from the shelter
Of the van; the car that hit
Her went no faster.

We put her on the sheets,
And gathered in the caravan
Our every last possession off
The hedges. The dogs
And horses roared blue murder
As the fire took the household

Down to bone-handled knives,
Her mother's crimson scarf,

Pillows the children fought with,
And the carved chairs we'd found
On the street in Cheltenham
And never traced an owner for.

Waiting in the Social Security
For 50p's, I kept thinking
Of a night when she woke up
Screaming 'The fire! The fire!
Mind my bed! Take my bed out
To the cool of the roadside!'

The Fool in the Graveyard

When we die, we help each other out
Better than usual.

This was his big day, and he was glad
His Dad was dead, because everyone,
However important or usually
Unfriendly, came up to him and
Solemnly shook his new leather glove
And said 'I'm sorry for your trouble.'
No trouble at all. All these people
Who normally made fun of him
And said, 'What's your name, Dan?'
And laughed when he said 'Dan' (wasn't
That right and polite?), were nice as pie
Today. He'd missed him going to bed
But they'd given him a pound and
An apple and told him a joke.

That made him laugh a bit.
Coming down the aisle, he'd been
At the front with the coffin on
His shoulder, and everyone
Without exception looked straight
At him, some of them nodding gravely
Or mouthing 'How's Dan', and even
Crying, some of them. He'd tried
To smile and nod back, anxious
To encourage kindness. Maybe
They'd always be nice now, remembering
How he'd carried the coffin. Outside

It was very cold, but he had on
The Crombie coat his Dad had bought.

The earth was always yellower
Here than anywhere else, heaped
Next to the grave with its very
Straight sides. How did they dig
The sides so straight? The priest
Led the prayers, and he knew most
Of the answers. Things were looking up.
Today he was like the main actor
In the village play, or the footballer
Who took the frees, or the priest
On the altar. Every eye
Fixed on him! It was like being loved,
And he'd always wondered what that was like.
It wasn't embarrassing at all.

Down Syndrome

i.m. Joseph Leary

Right from the cradle it had been observed
You didn't grasp fingers hard enough;
Your smiles came all too readily,
Dispensed without prescription.
But sleep well, Joseph, and don't weep
For your pale eyes or your weakness
For the truth.

Take consolation that it won't be you
That has to declare strategy
Or give the order to burn sprawling
Ranks of soldiers. You're not even
In the running, poor old Joseph,
In the competition to achieve
Such grand affliction.

Keep to your first love: inspire again
Someone to give you the front seat
And drive west with the radio blaring;
Left at the grotto through the rushy wastes
Where the weak heads of cotton
Barely survive the scattering breeze
Off Shrone Lake.

I have a plan: on Easter Saturday
We'll pull up by the verge where the view
Is longest across to the mountains
And listen out for the first willow-wrens.

We'll see the daffodils that come
Before the swallow dares and take –
Take what

That we would wish untaken?
Words, maybe, to straighten out
Your energetic tongue and our
Crookeder tongues, so between us
We can name the things worth naming
And cure our more aspiring
Elocutionary malady.

Esprit de l'escalier

I thought he was the gardener as he bent
Over the roses. Fingering for leaf-scars,
He told me of a loud continuous hum
Inside his head, which a knowing man
Had told him (in total confidence)
Came from the tension generated
By the conflict of two great powers.
What powers, the wise man hadn't said.
Stuck for an answer, I only thought of
Brain tumours and how these unbudded roses
Would fade upon his grave. But should have said
How wonderful it was what wise men knew
Denied the rest of us, and how the roots
Of roses live on through a hundred half-years.

Vanellus, Vanellus

When I'd forgotten them, you told me how
I saw them in the morning going to school,
Tattering down the sallow sky of winter.
Now I know them well: I see them every mile
By flocks and companies in roadside fields
As I drive onwards through these snowcast days
To sit at your bed evoking them for you.

Munster Final

in memory of Tom Creedon, died 28 August 1983

The jarveys to the west side of the town
Are robbers to a man, and if you tried
To drive through The Gap, they'd nearly strike you
With their whips. So we parked facing for home
And joined the long troop down the meadowsweet
And woodbine-scented road into the town.
By blue Killarney's lakes and glens to see
The white posts on the green! To be deafened
By the muzzy megaphone of Jimmy Shand
And the testy bray to keep the gangways clear.

As for Tom Creedon, I can see him still,
His back arching casually to field and clear.
'Glory Macroom! Good boy, Tom Creedon!'
We'd be back next year to try our luck in Cork.

We will be back next year, roaring ourselves
Hoarse, praying for better luck. After first Mass
We'll get there early; that's our only hope.
Keep clear of the car parks so we're not hemmed in,
And we'll be home, God willing, for the cows.

Lastworda Betst

So many ways (formal, political,
Witty) of writing poems not on the theme
Of dead parents, it's surprising how many
Have fallen into the trap. Odd too
To find on waking this anniversary
Morning my eyelids – tearless and well-slept –
Were hot to the touch. A *midrash*, maybe,
Whose prophecy is found twenty-four years
Back, at the March-wind final whistle
Of a football match when, dull and emptied
Like a flask, I watched the crush-barriers
Reappear among celebrating Cork fans.
Their voice rose up, leaving the cold body
With our small company. I've never heard
My Christian name without a start again
Since he stopped and shouted it, his last word.

A Noted Judge of Horses

The ache in his right arm worsening
Morning by morning asks for caution.
He knows its boding, cannot be wrong
About this. Yet he is more concerned
For the planks in the float that need
Woodworm treatment before drawing in
The hay, and whether the coarse meadow
Must be limed before it will crop again.

Still in the pallid dawn he dresses
In the clothes she laid out last night,
Washes in cold water and sets off,
Standing in the trailer with his eyes set
On the Shrove Fair. As long as his arm
Can lift a stick to lay in judgement
Down the shuddering line of a horse's back,
He'll take his chance, ignoring his dream
That before September's fair he'll be mumbling
From a hospital bed, pleading with nurses
To loose the pony tied by the western gate.

from
GUNPOWDER

The Rainmaker

In the café at Crewe, you can still feel
The old excitement of trains: a stranger's
Eye-contact, held guiltily too long.
But as the Bangor train-time approaches,
Gradually the glamorous melt away
For Lime Street, Euston or Piccadilly.
You take your seat alone, half-reading the paper.

At the second stop a man – knocking on:
Seventy if he's a day – steps carefully
Into the seat across from you,
With neat cap and blue Everton scarf.
He reaches inside his gaberdine mac
And pulls out a small book. I can see,
Without peering too obviously,
That it is the poems of Dafydd ap Gwilym
In Welsh. His lips begin to move;
His eyes never lift again. He must be
Going to Bangor too. Celtic Studies Dept.?
But no: at Colwyn Bay, above the caravans
And idle fairground stuff, he folds the book
Back inside his scarf and off he goes.

And at that moment – 4.30 p.m.,
On Friday, January the thirteenth –
The bleared weather that had effaced
The long and horizontal English midlands
Gives way to reaching bird-filled shores
Where ringed plover vies with lapwing
To catch your eye against the latening sun.

The Iron Age Boat at Caumatruish

If you doubt, you can put your fingers
In the holes where the oar-pegs went.
If you doubt still, look past its deep mooring
To the mountains that enfold the corrie's
Waterfall of lace through which, they say,
You can see out but not in.
If you doubt that, hear the falcon
Crying down from Gneeves Bog
Cut from the mountain-top. And if you doubt
After all these witnesses, no boat
Dredged back from the dead
Could make you believe.

Louisburgh

*Interest in the weather is only forgivable
in those who have to make a journey by sea.*
GERALD OF WALES

Only one photograph caught the spring
Of moment when the wave splash-broke,
Throwing an iridescent screen
Of lace that the world was green behind
In west Mayo. Around the corner
Lobster-pots stood cold and empty
On the pier, up for cruelty,
Exercising their right of silence.
Below them in the stiller water
Gross orange jellyfish closed and opened,
Engine-valves slowed nearly to stopping.

Hold them. Freeze as well the picture
Of the curlew's call above the grotto-rocks
Of sugar-bag blue-grey, and we could spend
For ever here. But already, now,
In Ireland, the rain's eavesdropping
On the silence. Guilt is sitting on
The cracked guttering, as if he owned
The place, smirking, watching the drip.
Before we're round the fjord in Killary Harbour,
He'll have tightened his hold, our only thought
Of slipping slates and mortar's deliquescence.

The Float

Who would put iron wheels under
A hay-car? On the outward trip
Seed-motes, steel rope-hooks, children
Teeth-jagged, unbalanced
Trampolinists in a vacuum-chamber,
Two inches off the boards.

On the way back
A cream yeast-loaf, risen over
The sides, sliding backstage
Through fern-and-briar curtains
Into the past, as now in the mirror
The car seems to disappear
Through its own rear-window
Into the car-wash tresses.

Have the Good Word

Those modern gods, the concentration
Camp authorities, when they had stripped
You of your clothes, would ask if you
Had some saving skill which might outweigh
In value the lead fillings in your teeth:
If you could sew, or type, or translate
From one useful language to another.

What I could offer them is the ability
To tell people what they want to hear:
That they will win the war, or that
Their names will go down in history
With honour; or that, after their deaths,
Mourners will kneel at their neat suburban graves,
Leaving bouquets and plastic immortelles.

Passive Smoking

The cows' repulsive body-heat
Kept the car warm through frosty nights,
Making it easier to start
For its spattering push up the passage.
Even so, my father sat for minutes
Every morning and stared out
With the engine running
And the carbon monoxide folding
Into the blackthorn mist.

I loved it. I stood at the back,
Breathing deep the scented poison
While his gaze travelled up Murt's field
To the mountains beyond.
What he saw nearer I don't know:
A pheasant sometimes in November;
Occasionally a cold fox; a neighbour
Spraying a grey liquid across the hedge?
But always the inexorable
Brown-green, rain-infected mound.

Perseids

The darkening shoreline cleared
As the first stars formed, so
Everyone went to the pub
To give the night a chance
To prepare its sky in peace
For these momentous guests.
Just after midnight, when
The meteor shower was forecast,
We came back out and waited
For our eyes to grow accustomed
To the dark, with our backs
To the smoked orange light
Indoors. But they never
Readjusted, however much
We strained and peered against
The cloud-cover. And then
Large drops began to fall,
The first thunder to roll
In the distance. One by one
They jumped across us, breaking
Against the ground, to denote
The passing or coming
Of what wet soul who could say.

The Sugawn Road

You're driving down the sugawn road,
Just before midnight, late July.
The mist from the Araglen below
Ribbons in white patches by.
Ahead you know, less than a mile,
Is the cross by Glash school, where
You have to turn left for home.
But, as the car hums through that air,
Suspended in the radio's music,
You might by fortune never reach it.

Ceo Draiochta (Magic Mist)

Leary sniffed the sweating wheat
Which had heated in the rick
That heavy autumn, reluctant
To dirty the machine with it.
But thirty men were gathered in the yard
And two fences had been levelled
For the thresher's awkward entry,
So finally he shrugged
And withdrew to the kitchen.

Nothing went right all day. Twice
The zipping drum was choked by sheaves
That skidded from their tyings
So the engine growled to a halt.
The home farmer, hurrying,
Shouldered the drive belt off
With his sack. And all through the day
The strange bright mist that the sun
Could not break through got heavier

And the gloss-painted orange boards
Got slippier. They were nearly finished,
The best made of a bad job, when Leary
Who'd been dozing by the fire until
He'd be called to end the operation,
Leapt to his feet, hearing two things:
The machine's bellow rapidly sinking
And a scream that those of us in school
That famous day heard from two miles away.

They ran in all directions.
John Tim Jack, seventeen stone,
Cleared two walls on his way home.
Our Tim crashed through the front door
And hid his face in his chaff-pierced sleeve
Crying. 'Matt Bridgie slipped into the drum.
His leg was taken off from the knee down.'

That was it really. A man passing
From town tied a belt around the leg
And administered a cigarette.
Pieces of rubber from the wellington
And clots of sock were scraped
From the hopper. Ultimately
Some compensation was paid, enough
For a rudimentary false leg
And a few rounds of drinks.
Matt showed signs of a latent
Family talent for composing verse,
And often sang well past closing time.

Nel Mezzo del Cammin

No more overcoats; maybe another suit,
A comb or two, and that's my lot.
So the odd poem (two in a good year)
Won't do to make the kind of edifice
I'd hoped to leave. Flush out the fantasy:
The mid-point being passed, the pattern's clear.
This road I had taken for a good byway
Is the main thoroughfare; and even that
Now seems too costly to maintain.
Too many holes to fill; not enough time
To start again. 'I wasn't ready. The sun
Was in my eyes. I thought we weren't counting.'

Soon we'll be counting razorblades and pencils.

Stealing Up

I've always hated gardening: the way
The earth gets under your nails
And in the chevrons of your shoes.
So I don't plan it; I steal up on it,
Casually, until I find –
Hey presto! – the whole lawn's cut
Or the sycamore's wand suddenly
Sports an ungainly, foal-like leaf.

Similarly, I'd have written to you
Sooner, if I'd had the choice.
But morning after morning I woke up
To find the same clouds in the sky,
Disabling the heart. But tomorrow
Maybe I'll get up to find an envelope,
Sealed, addressed to you, propped against
My cup, lit by a slanting sun.

Aurofac 20

The chemist's perfect hair and her scent of roses
As we drudged in on our farmer's errand,
Coughing inferiority. Pink lipsticks,
Sunglasses, kiss-curls on cards of hairgrips:
Exoticism, sweetening the imagination
In a wet March when stogged wellingtons
Were welded to mud: 'The calves have scour, ma'am.'

The smell of hayseed; thinking the echo
Of the hayfloat's stammering ratchet
Tuning in, then fading over the air.
That station, quick, again; lavender, pine
And blue-flush our stale reflections in the days
Of sprays of the scent of roses.

Heather

How noticeably she broke in
Upon my life, displacing
Its age-old denizens,
Family and fantasy.
Her hair no brushed sheen
But knuckled nuggets
Of twisted gules,
Sprung vibrant as her name-flower.

Not unaccompanied, but with a guest
Whose acquaintance is more often
Claimed than proved: a name
Much taken in vain.
Close the curtains, lest
The lamp she lit might pull
In from the summer night
Mysterious moths to make cotters in her hair.

Elijah on Horeb

The dog stood in the middle of the kitchen,
Eyes shut, thin tongue panting, slaver falling
Copiously, as the thunder reloaded to blast
The window-frames again. She must have seen
The stray that worried sheep tied up and shot.
And the lord was not in that.

Danny Regan took to going to Mass
In his old age after a scrawny tree fell
In a November storm, crushing the car bonnet
In front of him. For a week we lifted branches,
Reopening roads, still smelling the pine.
And the lord was not in that.

The day we climbed the Paps, we had been warned
Of rain moving in off the Atlantic.
Without explanation, it never came. We sat,
Sheltered by the summit-marking dug of stones,
Looking south-west to the inlet at Kenmare.
Then we moved out to feel the breeze's blessing.

Gunpowder

In the weeks afterwards, his jacket hung
Behind the door in the room we called
His study, where the bikes and wellingtons
Were kept. No one went near it, until
Late one evening I thought I'd throw it out.
The sleeves smelt of gunpowder, evoking . . .
Celebration – excitement – things like that,
Not destruction. What was it he shot at
And missed that time? A cock pheasant
That he hesitated too long over
In case it was a hen? The rat behind
The piggery that, startled by the bang,
Turned round to look before going home to its hole?

Once a neighbour who had winged a crow
Tied it to a pike thrust in the ground
To keep the others off the corn. It worked well,
Flapping and cawing, till my father
Cut it loose. Even more puzzlingly,
He once took a wounded rabbit off the dog
And pushed it back into the warren
Which undermined the wall. As for
Used cartridges, they stood well on desks,
Upright on their graven golden ends,
Supporting his fountain pen so that
The ink wouldn't seep into his pocket.

Romantic Love

I've never felt the same about your eyes
Since learning that it's superfluity
Of uric acid that causes their brownness.
If that is true, then the small sticking-plaster
Folded in your elegant right elbow
May not be what you say it is – the cover
Of a hole made in your vein by the needle
Of the blood-doctor – but the calculated
Seal of your addiction.

I'd have your brown eyes blue:
Blue as lobelia, or expensive iris,
Or as the night sky over London,
Or the light on the dashboard
That indicates the headlights are full on.

Second-Class Relics

Pilgrimage to Lourdes from Ireland is not to be classed as
foreign travel and therefore should not require a passport.
TADHG FOLEY

When John Tim Jack made his pilgrimage
To Lourdes, he never got as far
As filling the neighbours' bottles
With the healing waters, so on the way home
He stopped at the stream in Islandbrack
And filled them there. Grace and recognition
Followed just the same. In every household
The clear bottles shook a blessing
On the youngsters driving irresponsibly
To dances at the Mecca Ballroom
Or the Edel Quinn. Its efficacy
Seemed no less than the pink-crossed window
Of linen that had touched the bones
Of Philomena, or the Aero-like
Volcanic rock we brought from Iceland,
Or the chippings from the Berlin Wall
You see on many travellers' mantelpieces
These days. All are prayed to; who's to say
The water where the cattle wash their feet
Is not as curative as that where saints
Appear, or that the New Order will not start
Below the bridge where John Tim's pups were drowned?

'Ebbe?'

She used to say. Was always. Didn't like.
Such cold, novel preterites: not long since
She is and thinks and says. Always positive,
Active voice, imperfect, running with buckets.

On her birthday now my work goes well.
I don't need to get hot and irritated
Combing the unending remainder shelves
For Namier or the loves of Charles the Second.
She isn't waiting to enthuse too much
While warming to her theme, her eyes lighter blue
As she expanded, dwelling on the page.

Now I'd welcome the tedium of her History's
Excessive circumstantiality.
In this future perfect I wouldn't sigh.

Otter-Children

Where did I leave my cap? Some day
I must look. Maybe in the room
Where the stuffed otter twists to face you
In his cage of water. Once I or someone
Stood with a homemade drag-net,
Knee-deep, shifting in the river
After a flood, hoping to catch
The salmon and with him (who knows?)
Wisdom. I watched a dark shape
Speed downstream, then hit square on,
Causing me to lose footing.
And hat and bag and tackle.

The last time I ventured in the room
(You'll come in to look?) I thought I saw,
Hiding behind the arching couch,
Children – two, even three – laughing
And sly. When you look straight at them,
You see nothing. But when you face
The humbled water-dog's indignant glare,
You can sense them, like a migraine's shiver
In the top left-hand corner of your vision,
Laughing still but also holding out
A hand pleading with you to step across
The fire-screen, into their day beyond.

Neighbourhood Watch

The tinkers live beyond the verges
Of the town. Under cover of night
Their dogs scavenge from the dustbins,
Knocking the lids off. In broad daylight
They tether their ponies by our hedges.

The shopkeepers live lives of their own.
They pull down the blinds at 9 p.m.
To count their takings behind locked doors.
Their children often die before their parents
While business is creamed off by supermarkets.

The people live in the better parts of town,
With long lawns and variegated borders
Stretching down to the lane. They used to take
The tinkers' children in service by the year,
But now they're warier and make their own beds.

Going Without Saying

i.m. Joe Flynn

It is a great pity we don't know
When the dead are going to die
So that, over a last companionable
Drink, we could tell them
How much we liked them.
Happy the man who, dying, can
Place his hand on his heart and say:
'At least I didn't neglect to tell
The thrush how beautifully she sings.'

Áine

i.m. Áine Murphy, who died aged 5 months

Those rosebuds I brought away
From the room in the crematorium
Where your small white coffin
Slid from view, wilted
On the car's plastic ledge
While we ate and drank, all of us,
Mourning your taking off.
But two days later, look,
They're reaching up again
On a sunny windowsill,
Learning to stand
On stems, frail and graceful,
Pink bowls unbalanced
With perfect unease
On their long, green shoots.

Metamorphosis

A flower of spring, the lupin's gone by June.
Theresa brought them to us in four glass jars
On her way to school, and we planted them
Due west of the house. They were dwarf variety
With small pink and yellow flowers,
But twenty years later they were portly,
Swelling bushes, eighteen years after
Theresa herself had died of polio.

Now that another decade's passed, her children
Would be going to school and the dry seeds
That cracked in the pods refulgent,
So I have the heart to try again my hand
At lupins. And every morning, back here
In Knockduff, I'm woken at 4 a.m.
By a single agitated swallow,
Patrolling her alarm-calls up and down

The yard. When I pull the curtains open,
I can just make her out, flying fast
In wide ellipses, as if practising
For the long haul to Africa. Finally,
She alights straight overhead, her anxious
Insistent twitters settling into
The grace of a happy end with the fiddler's
Leaning down on the second-last note.

from
HERE NOR THERE

Nechtan

When Bran and his more worldly-wise companions
Were settling happily in the idyll
Of the Island of Women, I spoilt it
For them – and for me – by being homesick
For Ireland. But then we found there was
No longer any welcome for us there.
Maybe out of resentment for the months
We'd spent living in Love's contentedness,
They wouldn't let us land, so now we're fated
To sail for ever in the middle seas, outcast
Alike from the one shore and the other.

The Owls at Willie Mac's

Having heard their cries across the fields,
I went outside into their element,
As blind in theirs as they in mine by day.
It was so dark, that late summer night,
I could see nothing of what caused
The ticking, and the steady tread
Of heavy boots towards me down the road
Until his bicycle was right alongside.
Still without seeing, I could smell the warmth
And kind breath of Nugget Plug and Guinness.
And then the voice, as from an invisible flame:

'When I worked at Willie Mac's, you'd hear them
Every night. You'd never see them, even when
They were right on top of you and sounding
Like a screech of brakes.' Who was he,
This dark-dressed, nearly extinct escaper
From the nineteen-fifties Saturday night?

There are some animals, the medievals said,
Whose eyes are so acute that they can, lidless,
Outstare the sun. He walked away from me,
Saving the battery by still not winding on
The squat flashlamp I pictured at the front.
Neither could my defective vision see
Him as he would be three months ahead,
Stretched in the road like the thirsty bittern
By a car that could hardly be expected
To pick him out against a wintering sky.

Ghouls

I see in the mirror that they've stolen
The skin from my mother's grave – flaky,
Blotched, dried out – and pulled it down
Over my face like an old stocking
For disguise. They've used more of it
To cover the backs of my hands;
I see it tauten between index-finger
And thumb as I wriggle into
An invisible glove. It is like
The obscene-looking puckers forming round
The thick nub of a deflating balloon.

The gel I soft-soap between the palms
And over my face cannot disguise the fact
That these are secondaries: signs of
Deeper-lying things the face can't hide.

The Definition of Love

It's strange, considering how many lines
Have been written on it, that no one's said
Where love most holds sway: neither at sex
Nor in wishing someone else's welfare,
But in spending the whole time over dinner
Apparently absorbed in conversation,
While really trying to make your hand take courage
To cross the invisible sword on the tablecloth
And touch a finger balanced on the linen.

A young curate of a parish in West Cork
Was told his mother was seriously ill
And he must come home to Boherbue
(In fact she was dead already; they had meant
To soften the blow). He drove recklessly
Through mid-Kerry and crashed to his death
In the beautiful valley of Glenflesk.
This was because he fantasised in vain
About touching her fingers one last time.

The Faultline

When there's a sprinkle of snow
In mid-January, yet not enough
To stop it turning vein-translucent.
When young relationships freeze
And snap. When death, suddenly,
Crops up in the conversation
And no one quite remembers
Who raised the subject. As far past
Solstice as November was before it;
No sign of spring, and no
Going back. All just serving
To show, in case we'd forgotten,
Our faultline: that we're designed
To live neither together nor alone.

The Uvular 'r'

i.m. Joan Hayes

The City on Sunday morning: turf briquettes
And Calor-gas rounded up in network compounds,
And the mist so dense you can hardly see
The ochres and light greens of Sunday's Well
Across the river. We were the Cork crowd;
We always lacked the definition
Of the more western voice and land in Kerry.
The south Cork coast, kind and all as it was,
Wasn't Dingle. Our gaeltacht was speckled,
Consonants that compromised and faded
On the mouth's roof like Communion wafers.
That our bruachs were riverbanks; that our local names
Took the English word for it: Newquarter,
Watergrasshill and Coalpits and Halfway.

Pencil It In

Stumbling my fingers along the shelves,
I observe an interesting thing: books
I have had for more than thirty years
Feature my name in proud fountain pen.
Now I'm reminded of it, I recall
Practising on rough paper to reach
Such a convincing dash of signature.

For a while they went slantwise,
In legible ballpoint; then anywhere,
With any implement: rollerpoint, red even.
Recently I am perturbed to find
I've started to sign in pencil. HB,
Naturally; but will the time come
When less permanent leads will do?
2B, 3B, 4B . . .

A Fool at Doon Bridge

Et ai be faih co.l fols en pon
BERNART DE VENTADORN, *c.*1170

He couldn't wait for the swallows to come back,
So they sent him down to the Araglen Bridge
Where he'd last seen them, cutting low
Through the arches. 'The summer's nearly here,'
They said, 'so keep a close eye on the river.
As soon as you see it starting to slow down,
Get back quick and tell us, and we'll fill
Baths and buckets and kettles and warming-pans.'

He hung over the centre arch all day,
Watching the water carving its way down
Towards him. He saw the collies flickering
Invisibly in the mud, as good as mud
Themselves. Occasionally the level seemed
To drop, but when you closed one eye (like this)
And raised a finger, the brown hole in the bank
You measured it against didn't make a stir.

This was the place as well where he had seen
A dipper in the March flood working the silt
Beneath the rags of plastic in the blackthorn.
He'd just begun to remind himself of that
For comfort, when suddenly he spotted
The mocker in the branches overhead,
Tail bent downwards like a snapped twig. 'Look, Dan!'
He called to himself out loud, 'The cuckoo!'

Long Words

I can't remember what enterprise it was
We were breaking to each other
That made Denis John give me the word:
'My grandmother' (I knew her: a woman
Forever at her prayers) 'says
The longest word in the world is
Transcranscriptiation.'

So far I haven't found one longer than it,
For all my browsing in the Dictionary.
'Though I didn't go to school myself,'
The old people were fond of saying,
'Still I met the scholars coming home.'

The Mark of Cain

They misinterpreted My purposes
In imposing it. I'm not concerned
With Cain, with whether he's killed or not;
I wanted to demonstrate that people,
Without any written instruction,
Will look away: not mock; instinctively
Not maim those afflicted enough already.

But Cain did die. And woe to the hand
By which he died! Woe too to the day
When Cain woke to find the port-wine stain
Had vanished from his temple. For that's the day
They'll fall on him and rend him limb from limb.

Hermes

And now I long to be a poet
With something good to say.

i.m. Denis O'Connor, 1917–1997

Just as I'm happier walking in the dark
Of night and feel more safe in planes
Than on the ground, I'm less at ease
Among the living than the dead.
For years I've specialised in writing
Letters to the bereaved, a brief
From a licensed afterlife, consoling
Children, widowers and widows.

But who am I to write to about you,
Denis, who made your own way? I'd like
To honour your unrivalled singing,
Your melojeon, and your wit-barbs;
Your merriment among the dancers,
And your vamped mouth-organ. Who do I remind
How you could run up the twenty rungs
Of a ladder standing in the middle
Of the yard, our stilted boy?

You had the excitement of the hare,
And a like form, away from the everyday.
You had the fox's glamour, the perfectly
Made out-of-the-ordinariness
Of that thrush's nest, sealed with spit,
You showed us above the arum lilies.
We admired, but didn't understand

That you were Hermes, bearing messages
From the past, and must return, like summer
Out over the top of the fairy-thimbles.

Who dug your grave, Denis,
Since you dug everyone's?
Who carried your coffin?
There's no one in the parish
Who would not push to the front
Of the crowd to bear you.
Are we now at liberty to call you
Dansel, the venerated, unaccounted-for
Nickname of your family,
That no one spoke in your presence –
Out of some sentiment: tact? or fear?
Love maybe. In the silence
After your death, may we speak it now?

In the grave, shall all be renewed?
Your celebrity? Will this letter do?
No: by way of postscript I remind us all
Of a late-December night when you were old
And sick and looking for a drive
To help you get your messages up home.
It wasn't easy to make out what
You were mumbling, with the drink.
'Christmas is the worst time of all
For the person living on their own.'

Christmas

Despite the forecast's promise,
It didn't snow that night;
But in the morning, flakes began
To glide all right.
Not enough to cover roads
Or even hide the grass;
But enough to change the light.

'Dogs, Would You Live for Ever?'

Frederick the Great

She's bent at stool, as the saying is,
Next to her deathbed. Her arched back
Is like white fish
That has been too long in the fridge,
Greyed at the spine-bones.

Crying, she says 'This is the worst now.'
I say 'Of course it's not.
You did as much for children
Often enough.'

But of course it was: the scene
Comes back, untriggered, more
Rather than less often,
Oddly enough.

I'd prefer you to wait outside.

Femmer

for Eugene O'Connell

Despite its soft ephemerality,
They say the growth of elder is a sign
Of age-long human habitation.
Under the elders in our decaying farmyard
Stands the last sugán chair, rotted at all
Its skilfully carved joints, so the lightest
Tenant would cause it to collapse.

There's one like it in the dying house
Of Padraig O'Keeffe at Glounthane Cross:
Not our Glounthane, but the one near Cordal
Where my forebears came from. I stole from there
A small piece of lino, geography-shaped
Like the booty-map in *Treasure Island*,
Where it lay among foxed holy pictures.

The stairs are dangerous; and no matter
How hard you strain you can't fool yourself
Into hearing his spectrally played polkas there,
Even in that valley of ghost-houses.
You have more chance five miles east the road,
Up through the forestry where the Blackwater
Rises and you can imagine anything
In that wind that blows at you all the way
From the Atlantic which, astonishingly,
You can see: its last gleam of silver
Both at Tralee and off the Blasket islands.

Reaper-and-Binder

Voices were lost as the reaper-and-binder
Went clacketing past, spitting out at you showers
Of gold you embraced with your arms overfull,
So the sheaves slithered down from the grip of their
  bindings
As children, incompetent, slide out of jumpers.

At night on your pillow your ears went on singing
In time to its music by echo and echo
While your awn-scalded forearms still throbbed from
  its fallout.

Unknownst to the People

The small boy's clothes smelt terrible:
Goats, maybe pig droppings – or something worse.
We had to defumigate the car
After we'd unwisely picked him up
Out of the rain on his way to shop
In Carraiganima (where Art O'Leary
Met his poetic martyrdom).

A strange accent: north of England
Overlaid with the aspirates of North Cork.
He told us about his Mum and Dads,
And how they'd built the palisade themselves
From bits and pieces of discarded wood.

All that summer, though we never saw
The occupants, we watched the holding grow
In confidence on its small quarter-acre:
The washing hung to dry; plastic buckets
Lying round. And always the blue of woodsmoke.

When we came back next spring, the whole place
Was gone, only marked by soaking, charred wood.
A year later again, and green grass was growing
To the neatly locked gate at the roadside.
We asked around, but no one seemed to know
Where they had gone to, or why,
And everyone looked downward to the ground.

Reassurance

And from his death-bed, suddenly he said
At the end of a life of faith: 'Peggy,
I hope things are as we always thought they were,'
And she assured him that Heaven certainly awaited.

Personally, I hope not. Because, if Hell and Heaven
Are assorted by the just God we learnt of,
We can have little prospect of salvation:
We who have turned to the sports news,
Leaving the hanged girl from Srebenica
On the front page, just as before we watched
Without a protest while the skeleton-soldier
Burned by the steering-wheel on the road to Basra;
We too who are so sure about the frailties
Of those who failed to do anything about
The Famine, or who'd turn up the volume
To drown the clanking of the cattle-trucks
That pulled away eastward in black and white.

Redwings

What were they playing at, those strange thrushes
That crowded the ground with hardly more
Than a *peep!*, disguised as the greatest
Songsters of the spring? Maybe they were hatching
A plan to fool the first-winter calves
Who can't make out what's happened to the sun
Or why their grass has been reduced
To cold clumps of marram. They never died,
It seemed, but flew off in low sweeps
Over the neighbouring ditches, onward to
The cold foothills of the mountains,
Of Caherbarnagh and the Paps. 'Farewell,
Fieldfare!' we said to them and to their kind,
Not sure if it was a dream, their winter break.

Clara

To climb the mountain it's necessary to cross
From the reservoir behind Mountleader
Through a walled corner which appears to be
Both house and trees. You have to negotiate
A small window into a kitchen-copse
Where a sycamore is growing through
A hearthstone. Nobody seems to know
Who lived there, not even the old people
Whose grandmothers remembered when there were
Nine houses in the half-acre of elders
Behind the Old Screen. In the autumn,
If you stand very still and listen,
You can hear, you fancy, behind the rustling
Of the leaves in the endless westerly,
Women's voices, quietly about their business.

The Drummers

i.m. Angus Macintyre on 31 March 1995

The first twelve days of April are old March,
So from here we proceed with caution
For a while. Yet the fritillaries
Have already hung magic lanterns
From their green javelins, so it must be safe
For the roses to shoot again: those roses
That Angus mocked yearly because they put out
Elaborate mauve feelers before the last frost
And paid the penalty, like over-eager students
Rushing to judgement too enthusiastically.

The chiffchaff's back, early this year,
And the woodpeckers are drumming away.
For some odd reason, this morning
Those drummers, who normally startle
At the first sign of observation
And flee in disappointing lifts and swoops
Into the distance, hold their stations,
Beating a tattoo as if their lives
Depended on it. When my arms and neck ache
And I move on, they move ahead as well
And drum again before me, like scouts
With some message too urgent to ignore.

Westering Home

Though you'd be pressed to say exactly where
It first sets in, driving west through Wales
Things start to feel like Ireland. It can't be
The chapels with their clear grey windows,
Or the buzzards menacing the scooped valleys.
In April, have the blurred blackthorn hedges
Something to do with it? Or possibly
The motorway, which seems to lose its nerve
Mile by mile. The houses, up to a point,
With their masoned gables, each upper window
A raised eyebrow. More, though, than all of this,
It's the architecture of the spirit;
The old thin ache you thought that you'd forgotten –
More smoke, admittedly, than flame;
Less tears than rain. And the whole business
Neither here nor there, and therefore home.

Ter Conatus

Sister and brother, nearly sixty years
They'd farmed together, never touching once.
Of late she had been coping with a pain
In her back, realisation dawning slowly
That it grew differently from the warm ache
That resulted periodically
From heaving churns on to the milking-stand.

She wondered about the doctor. When,
Finally, she went, it was too late,
Even for chemotherapy. And still
She wouldn't have got round to telling him,
Except that one night, watching television,
It got so bad she gasped, and struggled up,
Holding her waist. 'D'you want a hand?' he asked,

Taking a step towards her. 'I can manage,'
She answered, feeling for the stairs.
Three times, like that, he tried to reach her.
But, being so little practised in such gestures,
Three times the hand fell back, and took its place,
Unmoving at his side. After the burial,
He let things take their course. The neighbours watched

In pity the rolled-up bales, standing
Silent in the fields, with the aftergrass
Growing into them, and wondered what he could
Be thinking of: which was that evening when,
Almost breaking with a lifetime of
Taking real things for shadows,
He might have embraced her with a brother's arms.

from
OUTLIVING

The Day I Outlived My Father

Yet no one sent me flowers, or even
asked me out for a drink. If anything
it makes it worse, your early death, that
having now at last outlived you, I too
have broken ranks, lacking maybe
the imagination to follow you
in investigating that other, older world.

So I am in new territory from here on:
must blaze my own trail, read alone
the hoof tracks in the summer-powdered dust
and set a good face to the future:
at liberty at last like mad Arnaut
to cultivate the wind, to hunt the bull
on hare-back, to swim against the tide.

The City at Shrone

A strange place for a city, Shrone, where
The mountain rain drifts along the western Pap
And the fields drain downwards to Rathmore.

Still, it is a strange city. One small house,
Single-chimneyed, whitewashed and tethered to
A disconnected ESB pole near the ramparts.

Half as old as time. The blessed virgin shelters
In her glass grotto, her blue mantle fading
Like the sky, the beads round her neck rusting.

Maybe, after all, it's not such a foolish place
For a city: its long-past citizens sleep well,
Unvisited by showers of high explosive.

In Millstreet Hospital

My cousin, they tell me, doesn't wake up much,
nor does she seem to see the green mountain
framed in the window of this chapel of ease
for travellers booked in for their long pilgrimage.
When I leave at the end of visiting hours
a small, tidy man is sitting by the door:
stick, well-knotted tie, watch-chain, tweed jacket.
He gets to his feet, raises his hat and enquires:
'Excuse my troubling you, but would you be
going anywhere near a railway station?'
The young smiling nurse bends over him,
and takes him by the elbow, saying:
'Maybe tomorrow, James. Maybe tomorrow
we'll take you to the station.'

Alzheimer Fruit

In that underworld you ambled off to
On your own, you must have drunk or eaten
Something prohibited so that your memory
Of this life faded. But where could that place
Have been? And what was the fruit? If we knew,

We'd go there with you, or for you, and put it back:
Whatever it was you ate or drank or brought away.
I dreamt I came upon you in the early hours
In your pyjamas, scoring a sheet of paper
Over and over with a highlighter pen.

'This pen's gone dry,' you said. 'I'm trying my best
To make it orange up this paragraph.'

A Candle for Dolly Duggan

Improbabilities of course, we all
know that: that this graceful taper
I force into the tallowed cast iron
beneath the *Assumption* in the Frari
could change the heavens, so that she
can pick up her cigarettes and lighter
to move on to a higher circle, as before
she moved, talking, through the lanes of Cork.

Sir Thomas Browne said there aren't impossibilities
enough in religion for an active faith.
So I'll go on spending liras and francs
and pesetas across the smoky hush
of Catholic Europe until she says
'That's enough', and then I'm free to toast
her in red wine outside in the sunlit squares.

'The Horse that Had Visions of Immortality'

for George Jack

The painting, you reminded us, was abstract,
So we have to close our eyes in front of it
Before we can see a pattern and a line
In the movement of its colours. A painter
In West Cork sets up her easel by the shore,
Then copies what she sees inland, knowing
That behind her there stretches out
An inexhaustible expanse of ocean.

Open your eyes briefly, and try again
With this children's game. You mark an 'x'
On a sheet of paper, and a dot
Four inches away from it. As you move
The paper in and out before your eyes,
Always intent upon the dot, the 'x'
First goes and then appears again.
Or a last Piers Plowman's look, *perceiving*

More deeper, at a clutch of daffodils
Which toil upwards from the thick twists
Of greenwhite at their base to the lipsticks
Of their careful, skin-packaged heads.
A few days on, most of the flowers are still
In bloom, but one or two are drying. Why?
Faced with that question, all that we can do
Is close our eyes and wait for another vision.

Telegrams

for Mick Henry

1 TWIST AND BUST

End of a day in the wet trench,
you're all so tired you can hardly pull
the boots off, but you have to
before the pub will let you in.
*Polite notice: site footwear
not admitted.*

On the dark table,
inside the digs' front door:
the buff envelope, face down.
Whose father, sister, brother, mother
this time? Come on; leave it. Eat first,
play a hand of cards in the Bell,
face it after closing-time.

2 DELIVERY BOYS

Fogarty's kept his usual station at the bar
all night, with a good view of the swing doors
in the mirror in front of him. Two more
and he'll be off himself to catch
the second-last bus to Camden Town.

And then he sees them coming: two
workmates from the old days in Bristol,
but wearing ties. 'I know what's bringing
ye fuckers, and I don't want to hear about it.'

3 SAILING TICKETS

In high summer when they all went home,
numbers on the mailboat were controlled
by the issue of ten-shilling sailing tickets.
No getting on without them: that is except
if you could show an Irish telegram
to the man at the barrier: 'I must get back
for the funeral, sir; my mother's passed away.'
Sometimes of course she had; more times she hadn't.

The Quiet Man

One of the great films, by general consent,
It could have been called 'The Quiet American',
Or, for that matter, 'The Violent Irishman':
Trim John Wayne, not easily roused, but once roused
His vengeance a wonder of the Western world,
With Maureen O'Hara, for all her wish
For independence, kicking impotently
On his shoulder. We saw it in Manchester,
On holiday from the hayfields of North Cork,
During the Korean War, at a time when films
Ran continuously. We came in, aptly enough,
At the culminating meadow fight,
Stayed for Tom and Jerry and the Pathé News,
Before leaving at the point we'd started at,
With McLaglan lying battered in the hay.

Two Fiddlers at Scully's

For the higher notes, the fiddle lifts Tim Browne
By the chin clean off his seat, like a child
Hoisted by the jowls to see France or China.
But not painfully: you can tell that
By the small smile that never leaves his mouth
And the readiness to laugh behind his glasses.
Raymond hardly stirs: his eyes never shift
From his fiddle which he scrutinises
In solemn puzzlement, nudging the music out
While Browne pulls it gallantly across himself.

No More Bother to Him

i.m. Paul O'Flinn

The red kites are very red this morning,
caught by the spring sun as they swing high
over Nuneham Courtenay, and in town
a wintered-over flycatcher skates out,
trying to keep his footing on the air.
So things are looking up at last it seems:
the floods receded, and the long winter's cold.

But on the eastern skyline, out past Bicester
a black pall hangs above the trees
where the cattle are burning, pyres no doubt
that we will see tonight replicated
over Tetovo on the News. There is
cause then for these red eyes all round,
light as Paul would have made of mourning him.

Concordiam in Populo

And Duncan's horses . . . 'Tis said they ate each other

After the heart attack, prodigious events
Took place: neighbours who hadn't talked
For twenty years, because of trees cut down,
Horses gone lame, or cattle straying,
Cooperated in organising lifts
To make arrangements for the funeral.

Husbands who'd not addressed a civil word
To wives for even longer referred to them
By Christian name in everybody's hearing:
Lizzie or *Julanne* or *Nora May*.
The morning of the burial it rained and rained.
And we all huddled close by the graveside,

Trusting one another, small differences
Set aside, just as Kate had told us once
How she crept into bed when the thunder seemed
To throw giant wooden boxes at the house,
Beside the husband that she hadn't spoken to
Since the first month after their sorry wedding.

Philomela

If things got any worse, she'd take up knitting
and sit across the hearth from his thin-lipped silence,
murmuring a new language and logic:
Cast on purlwise. Knit one stitch through back
of loop. Yarn around needle. C6B, P6, K2.
And it would all mean nothing to him,
such woman's writing. No more than love had.

So what should the picture on her peplum be?
On the whole, a sorry scene: not exactly
a tongue cut out, but the steady rooting up
of a grove of voices, one after the other.
And as her fingers filled the details in,
his hawkish eyes will fill with tears, hearing
her absent humming from across the fire.

Growing Up with Cullen Feis

The heel-to-toe batter of the hammering hornpipe
Mutes by a swift Cinderella-change to cross-garters
For the high-leg-reaching, silent reel, as if
The feet's speaker has suddenly gone dead.
Tension mounts: the bitter flusteredness
Of the dancing mothers – *Majella! Where's your cape?* –
Urging back more and more from the Coal-Quay call
Of the tinkers' stalls – 'Apples and oranges
And ripe bananas!' – as the crimson-Celtic, ringleted,
Bone-kneed small girls grow through the evening
Into the distant, black-stocking hauteur
Of the long, long-legged senior teenagers.
The judge is incorruptible, undistractable,
His eyes fixed low on the yielding ash-boards,
Sprung like a good hurley. The heartbeat
Of the accompanists never falters either.
Unchanging too the backdrop to Singleton's field:
Caherbarnagh in Munster blue, Clara greener,
And the mocking conic profile of the Paps.

Shells of Galice

I like to set this modest test for scientists
who'll follow after, to wash some influence
into the future. I carry shells from one
seashore to another: from the Atlantic sweep
in front of the Riazor Hotel, beneath
the excited lights of Deportiva,
to hide them in the silence of Dunquin

or on the cold, eastward-facing coast
of Lindisfarne. I've left Irish mussel-shells
exposed to the midday sun at Ostia.
Once I placed a pale-pink sea urchin
with all its fragile porcelain-like stipples
to take its chance high on a limestone mountain.
How are they going to account for it,

archaeologists in the years to come?
Will they guess that someone intervened
and tampered with geology's design,
the no-pace-perceived drift of continents?
Or will they see a different pattern in it,
how love and whim and irrational attachment
make us keep moving things from place to place.

Rhubarb, Rhubarb

We went up to Rockchapel, the two of us,
myself and Paddy Hickey; and because
he arranged a drive back with someone else,
I came home early, only stopping
at Curtin's shop to buy a bunch of rhubarb.

Still all right: still before the end of July
when rhubarb turns bitter and the days
get shorter, and well before you start
to count the dates from the darkening evenings
to the end of summer when they put back up

the big green wood shutters in Normandy
and children face for school again, and you throw out
July's *Irish Times* at the end of August.

The Company of the Dead

It's natural that they would feel the cold
much more than we do; but that is partly
what makes them such good company.
They draw closer, rubbing their hands,
and praise the fire: 'That's a fine fire you've down.'

Also, they've no unrealised agendas,
their eager questions no barbed implications.
They're no trouble round the place, their only wish
now to get warmer: apart, that is, from wishing
that they'd kept warmer while they had the chance.

Islandmagee Castle

for James Simmons

It is a castle, according to the map,
and you can find your way to it by climbing through
from the Crawfords' cattle-sheds. Right enough,
it has a Norman-looking arch over the gap
which must be where the window was, though now
it's just six feet of stone, barely hanging
together. The calves are nudging at
the hay-wisps round its base, oblivious to

what lies behind them: oyster-catchers
crying down at the shingle beach; sheer blue
between them and the green of Portmuck island,
and Ailsa Craig beyond. Once I stumbled
through there, trying to keep my feet, and found myself
face-to-face with a furtive-looking character,
his double-breasted coat hugged close around him.
'A gun,' I thought. He opened his coat

revealing a colander of mushrooms.
'Take as many as you want for your Ulster fry,'
he said. 'Sure the fields are full of them this weather.'

Goalkeepers

Custodians. The last line of defence,
Most celebrated lineage of heroes.
Tony 'The Dummy' Reddan of Tipperary,
Whose farm-cap kept the sun out of his eyes
So the ball thumped safely into his heart
Of blue and gold where his generous hand
Could close on it. Art Foley of Wexford
Who made the great save from Ring in '56.
Kilkenny's all-time All-stars, Walsh and Skehan.

When I first read the papers, Cork's goalie
Was a legend whose brother I got to know
In Oxford a generation later.
He lived towards the bottom of Divinity,
In a houseful of quiet, single, courteous,
Drinking Irishmen. He never boasted of
His celebrated brother: even discouraged
Talk of him. And one cold January night
He jumped from Folly Bridge into the Thames.

Finnéigeas

Though failing in his lifelong quest for wisdom
when the boy burned his finger on the salmon
and licked the pain, he got the better bargain
in the end. For, in his declining years,
it was his fireside that friends gathered by
to listen to the learning of his failures,
while know-all Finn, after whom were named
mountain ranges and battlefields, was hated
by all for the miseries he caused and suffered,
and there was praise only for the man who'd kill him.
And ultimately Finn's wisdom told him this:
no one loves a wise man, not even himself.

Sedge-Warblers at Beckley, June 2002

for John and Jean Flemming

This terrible summer, we must make the most
of every sunlit evening. So we walked
by the new fibre track above the reeds,
mocked by their extraordinary goat-song,
so unlike the song of birds. And such odd
accompanists: free of all shyness,
they'd start to call when we came within earshot,
untroubled by our talk or peering for them,
and stop, disappointed, as we left.
Sometimes we would watch the reeds swaying,
sure sign of their presence, a sign of life,
but never the birds themselves: strange acrobats
that made their long poles waver at the top
by swinging at their base. Or so it seemed.

Two larks filled with their back-dreaming song
the central space marked out by church steeples:
Islip and Addington and Fencott.
Even shaded eyes could not pick them out,
well as the sound located them. But if
you half-closed your eyes, as once you did
to spread the light of candles in the church
from oval glow to stretched-out yellow pool,
you had a better chance of seeing them:
just to one side of where the unbroken rapture
seemed to come from, a few degrees away,
a dancing point, a concentration of
the cloud. No more than that, yet everything
your eyes' attentiveness had reached out for.

Any Last Requests

i.m. Padraig Ó hIcí

But I was here on Broadway,
Carrying bricks for load,
When they carried out her coffin
Down the Old Bog Road.
THERESA BRAYTON

This sunny October morning, I notice
for the first time that the swallows are gone,
well gone, though I never saw them going.
I'm busy brushing wood preservative
into my English garden fence, while you
are being driven for the final time,
down from Eagloune, past the ditch where
on party nights it was so dark
the shushing visitors couldn't find their cars.
I should be driving with you
past your untended loganberry beds,
to negotiate the dangerous northward turn
by the forge. It no longer matters
that the wind gets through the broken panes
which you had better things to do
than to get fixed. I think
it no longer matters; but then I'm not there.

No other house where I was
so unconditionally welcome,
even after failing you in one of your
far-fetched lifelong enterprises:
your strange soprano 'hello' always

a misleading prelude to the letters
you rooted for under the *Saols* and cushions
and books and *Examiners*. And every time
I failed to visit, no less welcome
the next time. But what happens now?
When I next push my way past the dog
and turn the key that is always in the lock,
I will at last be greeted by silence.
'*Bhfuil tú sa bhaile a Phádraig?*
Are you home?'

Vanishing-Points

for Robert and Badral Young

Safe in an armchair in the dentist's surgery,
you observe your daughter's treatment:
being cruel to be kind again. You fix on
the criss-cross of her trainers' soles
in the foreground, on past her brave socks,
grazed knees, school jumper and clasped hands
to the vanishing-point that is her head,
laid back. It is the same perspective as
in the photograph of the thrown-away body
of the young Taliban soldier. His trainers,
similarly foregrounded, look as if
they could be the same designer label.
But this vanishing-point is past his head, way out
in the impassive desert sands towards Kabul.

The Mule Duignan

Nowadays it always rains in Bristol,
and every night, trying to get to sleep,
I hear it, looking beyond to the lights
winking over the Clifton Bridge, like the lights
of the shoreline seen from the Irish mailboat.

It helps me to drop off if I go over
details from childhood, like the big key
of acrid cast iron that shut and opened
the front door. I find it strange to still remember
that it opened clockwise, and locked the way
you'd expect to open it. Most often
I think back to a December night
when my small sister crept into bed with me,
shivering. We listened to our father's voice,
emphatic and quiet: 'If the cow does die tonight,
we'll have to sell up and go.' We prayed ourselves
to sleep. In the morning the wind woke us
and we all went out together to the stall.
The cow was standing up, eating hay.
And then for the first and only time I saw
my parents embracing. I hate that country:
its poverties and embarrassments
too humbling to retell. I'll never ever
go back to offer it forgiveness.

When my father died at last, the place
was empty. I went back to bury him,
then turned the key in the lock and dropped it
in the estate-agent's letterbox
and turned my back for ever on it all.

[117]